The library of
Stable Management

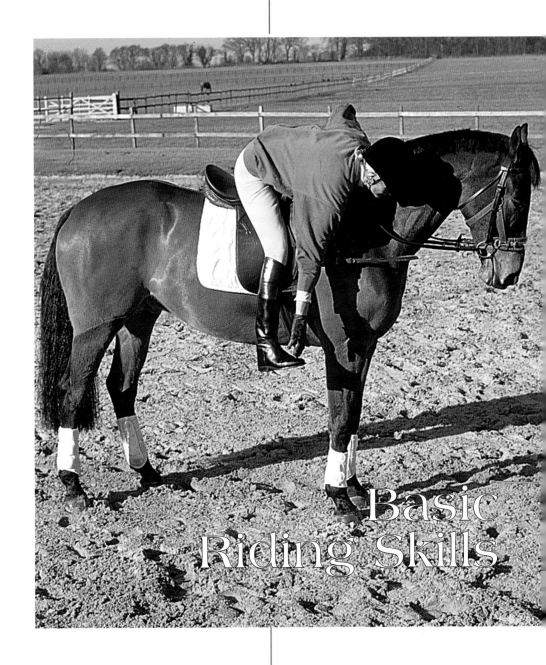

Basic
Riding Skills

Mark Hallion
and Julie Langrish

The library of Stable Management
Basic Riding Skills

Contents

The authors would like to thank the following for their help:
- Malcolm Dunning Saddlery
- Jeremy Mantell MRCVS
- Mrs. Gillian Knight and Mrs. Yvonne Bryant for modelling

Chapter One

Introduction

 Developing the young horse from the initial backing is the most interesting and important stage of all. Correct training now is the basis of its future.

Time and commitment are essential and you should not consider training the young horse if you only have limited time available.

Each horse is an individual and some take longer than others, both mentally and physically, to achieve what is required of them. We are talking years, not months.

Let us start at the point where the young horse is just backed. It is three years old. It has accepted the rider and is walking and trotting around the field.

At this stage, it has not developed strong muscles and so you have to be very careful not to overdo the training, which will cause tiredness and put unnecessary strain on the horse's limbs and body. Depending on its physical state at this stage, a maximum of half an hour is all that you should ask of it. Work out a programme which fits into your own life style so that you can progress consistently with the training.

The young horse should be worked six days a week. At this point you need to plan ahead. You might consider working it up to a stage after which you wish to turn it away for a short time to mature.

I think it is best to back the young horse in the spring and work it lightly in the summer and autumn. Then turn it away through the winter months when the weather is colder, the days are shorter and the conditions not so good for work. The following spring, the horse will be four years old and able to cope with more work.

Alternatively, start the backing in the autumn, carry on through the winter and do not turn away. It all depends on the horse's mental and physical well-being. As long as you are asking no more than your young horse is able to cope with then you will do no harm.

Be prepared to give your horse the time it needs. A horse will tell you what it can and cannot cope with and it is very important to develop a sensitivity so that you can understand this.

Teaching the young horse to go forward freely is a combination of correct schooling and riding out on the lanes. Too much intensive schooling day after day can lead to mental and physical strain. Nowadays, riding out on the roads can be unpleasant and dangerous due to the increase in traffic. If you are fortunate enough to have tracks and quiet lanes on your doorstep, then nothing could be better for the horse and rider.

Ideally, I would school the young horse

Just backed, relaxed and walking out.

have the time, don't buy a young horse. As stated previously, half an hour's schooling is all that a young horse can cope with in the early stages. Build up to an hour's ride on the lanes if possible. Try to find someone with an older, sensible horse to accompany you on your rides out. It is not wise to take a three-year-old out on the roads alone. When it understands about cars, lorries and various other surprises then it may start to go out alone, but don't be in a hurry to do this. Build up its confidence and trust and try not to let it get frightened. Let it follow the older horse past things that may worry it. You will soon find that it will be quite happy to lead the way if it has not been frightened and forced past too early.

Road work is vital for all horses because it encourages forward thinking, keeps the horse's mind fresh, builds up stamina and muscle and, most of all, is enjoyable for horse and rider. However, if you live on a busy main road then it is not advisable to have a young horse.

Depending on the progress of the young horse, you may feel that it would be wise to lunge it for ten minutes before you ride. This may be beneficial if your mount is

three times a week, alternating this with a hack out between schooling sessions. Three hacks, three schools and one day off a week. Of course, the horse should be turned out for a few hours every day if possible. Be careful not to leave your young horse out too long in cold and wet weather or if it is very hot. Some people think that horses need to be out for long hours to settle them down, but, in fact, this can have a reverse effect.

Ideally, work your horse in the morning and turn it out in the afternoon. If possible, try not to leave it totally out at grass; it cannot possibly cope with the work on a continually full stomach and can never become adequately fit. This all needs to be carefully worked out before you commit yourself. So many young horses are ruined due to lack of forethought. If you do not feeling bright as it does not do any good to either you or your horse if you get bucked off.

How much should be asked of the young horse when it is being schooled? This all depends on the individual horse. I cannot emphasise too strongly the need for experienced help from a good trainer. If you have this, then good progress should be made in the horse's own time. Horses are like children, some can be quick to learn and others much slower. Give them the time they need. You need feeling and patience to understand when the young horse is struggling and not to ask for more than it can reasonably give you.

Of course, resistances need to be worked through but the reason for any resistance needs to be fully understood. A young horse's teeth are constantly erupting and their gums can become swollen and sore. Ask your vet to check your horse's teeth every six months to rasp any rough edges and remove wolf teeth (these are tiny extra teeth that appear just in front of the front molars). The removal of wolf teeth is a minor procedure but you will not be able to ride the horse for 7–10 days in order to allow the mouth to heal. You could plan to have these done when you are going on holiday or when you would like to give your horse a break. If left in, these teeth are a nuisance and the horse can fiddle about in the contact causing a noisy mouth.

The basic principles need to be taught to the young horse from the beginning – start

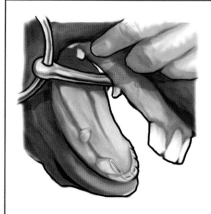

Tiny wolf teeth sometimes erupt close to the first of the molars or cheek teeth. If the gum is inflamed or they interfere with the bit, they must be removed.

Wolf teeth should be extracted by your vet. Large wolf teeth may require surgery.

Fault: nose in front of the vertical.

Correct outline: horse's face is vertical to the ground.

as you mean to go on. It needs to be taught to move forward and straight. These are two very simple words but so often are misunderstood by the rider. It should accept the hand and by this I mean that it accepts a firm hand but allows contact and responds to the leg aids. Do not expect too much impulsion to begin with. Impulsion is controlled energy and something that develops over a period of time. Feel softness and correctness in the pace, allowing the horse freedom and time to develop energy within the step. Remember, it has to develop strong enough muscles to carry the rider and a great deal of time and patience is required. The rider needs to understand fully from the trainer the right way to train the horse. There are certain words and phrases that must be completely understood by the rider which I will explain as simply as possible.

Tempo

The speed at which the horse travels. Too fast, and it is running forward out of rhythm, falling onto the hand and unable to relax in an outline. It will struggle to turn its body and fall out on the corners of the school. Too slow, and it will barely be able to keep in rhythm, feeling sluggish and, again, unable to maintain the contact due to its hind legs being insufficiently active.

The tempo may vary according to the horse's progress. Your trainer will see from the ground how to gauge the tempo and whether the step needs to be quickened or slowed down.

Rhythm

A regular consistent step within the correct speed. Some horses are naturally rhythmical as are certain people. The rider must learn to recognise lack of rhythm. Loss of rhythm may be due to incorrect speed, weakness or lack of muscle.

Activity

You feel that the horse is going somewhere but not in a hurry. Be careful not to hurry the young horse, particularly at the walk, because this takes time to develop. Activity and impulsion do not mean the same thing. Impulsion is developed from a slow stride later on in the development of the pace. The rider is educating the horse to flex the joints and be able to step higher off the ground in a controlled and effortless way. If the rider has too much activity, the horse loses its balance by rushing on to the forehand, being unable to sustain the lowering of the croup which enables the feeling of impulsion to come through to a lightened forehand. This is the ultimate and, of course, in the early stage of training the horse's balance is more on the forehand. It is only through correct and progressive training that the horse learns to shift that balance on to the haunches.

Straightness

The horse's hind legs should follow the line of the forehand, whether on a circle or straight line. The wither should stay central between the rider's hands. So often, the crooked horse falls onto the outside shoulder (falling out) or, due to lack of correct flexion, falls onto the inside shoulder, which creates the feeling of being on a motorbike going round a bend. The young horse will not move straight on its own. It needs consistent help from the rider to guide it correctly around corners and keep it straight on the circle.

In maintaining the correct speed and controlling the amount of bend in the head and neck, the young horse learns to move forward and straight. It must be taught to flex to the inside but not be allowed to overbend the head and neck to such a degree that it cannot control its shoulders. If the horse is losing the quarters to the outside it may help to straighten the neck, thus keeping the withers central and enabling the horse to control the haunches.

Lateral flexion

Lateral flexion is the development of the bend through the head, neck and body to the inside or, as in counter-bend, to the outside. The degree of this bend is controlled by the rider who must feel how much flexion the young horse can cope with whilst remaining straight and correct. Teaching the young horse to stretch down and around to the inside with its head and

Allow the horse freedom through the neck.

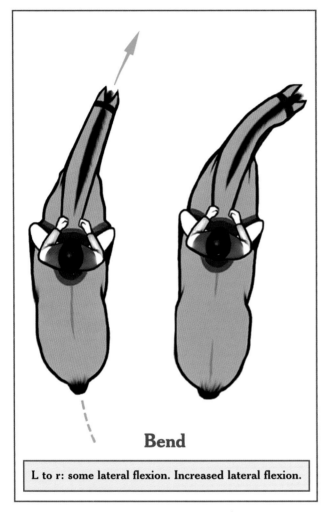

Bend

L to r: some lateral flexion. Increased lateral flexion.

secure lateral flexion in that the horse gains in confidence to stretch the head and neck, allowing the hind legs increased freedom. As the horse becomes stronger, it learns to activate the hind legs, thus lowering the croup and is able to lighten the forehand, allowing true impulsion to be developed.

The basic training of the young horse is vital even if you want only to hack out. Whether you are interested in dressage, show jumping or cross country riding, the young horse should be trained correctly from the beginning. Even if you are not an experienced rider it is possible to bring on a young horse providing you have consistent help from a good trainer.

neck but, at the same time, controlling its body to stay straight on the circle, enables it to open the shoulders. This will loosen the withers, poll and jaw which, in turn, allows it to stretch the top line and allows the hind legs to step under. This flexion should be encouraged on a straight line as well as a circle and through the corners.

The length bend is developed from

Not only the horse but the rider needs to be educated, so now we shall move on to what is required of the rider.

The basic seat

2 As a rider, you must learn to sit correctly so that you do not hamper the horse's movement. Learn to develop a soft but effective seat but, remember, this can take years to establish! It is never too late to learn to ride providing you have a sympathetic and knowledgeable trainer.

Make sure the saddle fits you and the horse. It is impossible to sit correctly if the saddle puts the rider in the wrong position and is either too large or too small. A dressage saddle is ideal but a good general purpose one will be adequate to begin with.

Sit with your body weight positioned centrally over both seat bones. Your upper body should feel tall from the waist up so that your neck stays close to the back of the collar. Your chin is raised slightly and your eyes looking in the direction of movement and not down at the horse, which is a bad habit to develop. The shoulder should be in line with the hip and the hip in line with the heels.

The leg should feel loose from the hip, with the knee bent and the foot resting in the stirrup on the ball of the foot with the toes directed forward and neither turned in nor

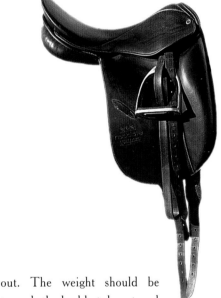

out. The weight should be towards the heel but do not push the heel down. As long as the toe and heel are level, that is adequate at beginner stage. As more strength and suppleness develops in the rider's legs, the heel will stretch down more easily but should never be forced.

If the seat bones remain relaxed, you will be able to keep the hips loose so that the large thigh muscle does not roll underneath the leg causing the knee to grip up and tighten the leg.

To begin with, you will find this position

Chapter Two

Rider demonstrating correct position.

difficult to control until you are supple and soft enough to absorb the movement of the horse through the hip joints, enabling the legs to relax. There are some very good suppling exercises for the rider to help overcome these problems (see pages 16-17).

Your upper body should remain as quiet as possible. Relax your shoulders and keep your elbows bent to allow the arm to move away from the body, giving the horse freedom of the neck and head. Hold the reins firmly, with the rein through the fourth and fifth fingers. Carry the little finger under the thumb. If the hands turn over the wrists can cause a block in the rein contact to the mouth. Keep the thumbs on top of the reins and treat your arm as an extension of the rein. Allow your elbows to move backwards and forwards, giving with the natural movement of the horse's head and neck.

Imagine a straight line – elbow, wrist, bit

– and control the horse with your fingers on the rein through an elastic contact to the horse's mouth. This takes time and practice and, ultimately, is the key to artistic riding.

So many horse problems are due to the rider's deportment, with the rider blaming the horse for resisting. Sadly, stiffness and lack of feel in the rider often cause the horse to be misunderstood. Even the most experienced riders need someone on the ground to remind them to stay in the right position so that they can concentrate on keeping the horse correct.

Lunge lessons are ideal to educate the rider to sit correctly. The lunge horse must be safe and well schooled so that the rider feels safe and secure. The rider on the lunge can concentrate fully on sitting correctly without the worry of controlling the horse in the early stages of learning.

The Rider's Position at Walk

Maintain the basic seat position, allowing the arms to move away from the body, following the movement of the horse's head and neck. Maintain contact with the lower leg close to the horse's sides and let the body move from the hip without excessive pushing from the shoulder.

Common Faults: The rider shows too much movement in the upper body and not enough movement through the arm. The contact should be maintained with a feeling of elasticity and the horse kept straight in

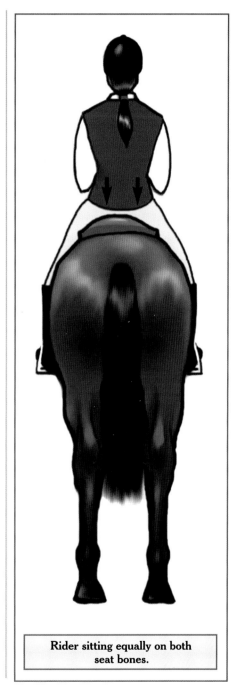

Rider sitting equally on both seat bones.

Rider maintaining correct position whilst allowing the horse to change his outline.

the correct bend. Too often the contact is insecure and the horse allowed to slop along. The trainer must check from behind that the rider is sitting straight with his weight remaining central.

The Position at Rising Trot

When a horse trots, its legs move in diagonal pairs in two time. The rider is rising on one diagonal pair and sitting on the other. Your seat should come off the saddle as little as possible so rest your feet in the stirrups, letting your knees and hips absorb the movement.

The hips move backwards towards the hands. Keep your knees bent so that the lower leg does not come too far forward. This will cause the knee to lock and force you to pull yourself out of the saddle.

When first learning to rise to the trot, it is helpful to lean forward slightly, which will stop you from losing balance and getting left behind. Once you have learned to sit and rise in rhythm with the horse's step then you must sit upright and learn to control the sit and rise through your hip.

Your hands do not feel so much head and neck movement as with the walk but you must be ready to allow any stretching forward of the head and neck if the horse wishes to do so. Remain upright but allow your arms to move away from your body when necessary.

The novice rider should not sit to the trot with stirrups until he is sufficiently supple to absorb the horse's movement and then only on a comfortable and well-schooled horse for short periods of time.

To train the horse correctly, the rider needs to develop a soft and supple seat which can take years, depending on the rider's natural ability. He needs to be able to ride the horse forward into an allowing hand. The horse is rewarded by a hand that yields. That is why the lunge is so beneficial in teaching the rider to maintain an independent seat.

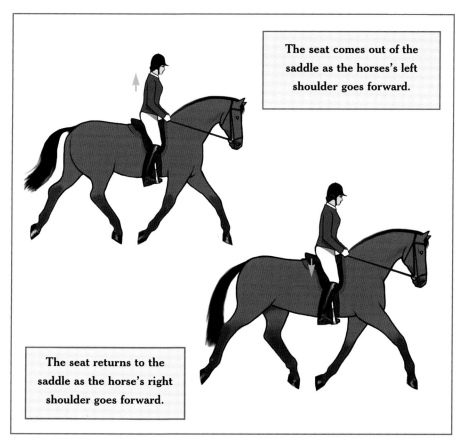

The seat comes out of the saddle as the horses's left shoulder goes forward.

The seat returns to the saddle as the horse's right shoulder goes forward.

Chapter Three

Exercise on the lunge

There are some very useful exercises to help make the rider's joints supple. Be careful not to overdo the exercises at first. Build up gradually to prevent undue strain on the muscles. Tie the reins in a knot so that you feel you can regain some control if things go wrong. The horse on the lunge should have side reins to help maintain the position of its head and neck. Therefore you can let go of the reins which normally stay in place. A neck rein may be used if needed.

On the lunge, try to follow the horse's shoulders with your shoulders and keep your hips level with the horse's hips. Look forward and around the circle. To begin with, warm up with stirrups at a walk and trot and start the suppling exercises when you are feeling relaxed and secure. Take the stirrups away once you feel safe and confident.

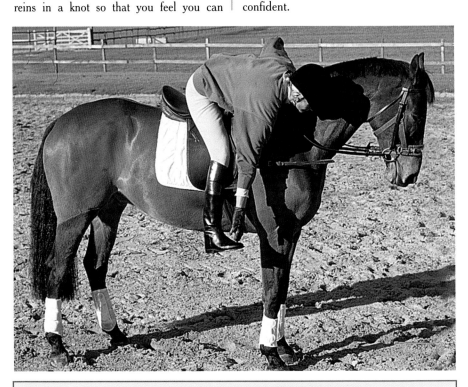

The author instructing on the lunge.

Rider performing suppling exercises.

Start the exercises at the walk. Hold the saddle with your outside hand, fingers just resting on the pommel. Your inside arm is now free and should hang down, fingers open. Keep the knees and thighs as loose as possible, let the toes drop down with relaxed ankles. Do not try to push the heel down; as you become more confident, it is more a case of raising the toe slightly.

*1. Make large circles with the inside arm, keeping the arm straight, fingers stretched and rotating the arm backwards. This will loosen the shoulders. Look straight ahead at all times. Make six arm swings

backwards with the inside arm and then hold on with the inside arm and repeat the exercise with the outside arm. Try to maintain the correct position of the leg throughout this exercise, keeping the lower leg close to the side of the horse.

2. Hold the saddle with the outside hand. Move your shoulders up and down or in a circular motion to release tension. Make circular movements with your head very slowly and just a few times.

3. Stretch both arms out to the sides at shoulder level and swing the arms to the left and right, turning from the waist. Repeat six times. The lower half of the body should remain in position when working the top half of the body and vice versa.

4. At the halt, stretch the inside hand above the head. Bend forward and down and touch the inside toes. Repeat three times. Do the same with the outside hand to the outside toes. Be careful not to let the free leg slip back; it can be difficult to control.

5. Raise the right arm above the head, bend forward and touch the left toe. Repeat twice more and change arms. If you can manage this at halt, you can then try it at a walk.

17

6. This is one of the best exercises at the walk. Raise both hands above your head, looking up at them. Feel your shoulders sitting over your seat bones and allow your hips to move underneath you. Slowly lower your arms, trying not to let your shoulders flop forward otherwise you will lose the hip movement and become too active with the upper body.

*7. Lift one leg, knee bent up, towards the withers, kick back and down opening the hip joint. Repeat three times with each leg.

8. Lift one leg, knee bent. Take the leg away from the saddle and place it back again, in almost a circular motion. The upper body may be

Rider stretching back with the left arm.

slightly behind the vertical, which will help. These leg exercises help loosen the hip joint and control the legs.

*9. Swing the lower leg back and forwards from the knee. Next, swing both legs together, with one going forwards and one going backwards.

10. The best exercise, which is quite difficult at first, is to straighten your knee and slide the leg back and forwards from the hip. Keep your upper body straight and see if you can slide the leg almost off the back of the

Stretch both arms out to the sides at shoulder level and swing the arms to the left and right, turning from the waist. Half a dozen times is quite adequate at this stage.

flap and then forward. Keep your seat bones in contact with the saddle.

*11. Turn the toes inwards in large circles and then outwards to loosen the ankles.

When you feel secure, the exercises marked with a star can be done at the trot. Half an hour on the lunge for horse and rider is adequate as it is extremely hard work. Finish the lesson by taking back the stirrups. You may feel it is necessary to lengthen the stirrups, which is a good sign. You should always feel comfortable with the length of the stirrups – it is better to ride a little too short than too long when you are learning. If the stirrups are too long you will lose control of the lower leg.

Once you have learned to sit correctly then you will be able to apply the aids in a quiet and effective manner.

Chapter Four

Applying the aids

The rider uses the lower legs close to the horse's sides to ask the horse to move forward; the hand to control the bend and pace; the voice to soothe or command; and weight which has great influence over the control of the steps.

The whip should be only be used to reinforce the leg aids when necessary.

The Leg Aids

The rider's inside leg stays forward on the girth area where the horse is most sensitive. The legs should stay in close contact with the horse's sides at all times but not grip. The inside of the calf squeezes the horse forward when needed. The outside leg may come a little further back behind the girth to control the quarters if necessary.

The inside rein asks for bend and direction. Once achieved, soften the inside rein, letting the horse yield to the hand.

The outside rein must be constantly secure and supportive. This rein controls the pace and asks for the half halt.

Medium walk.

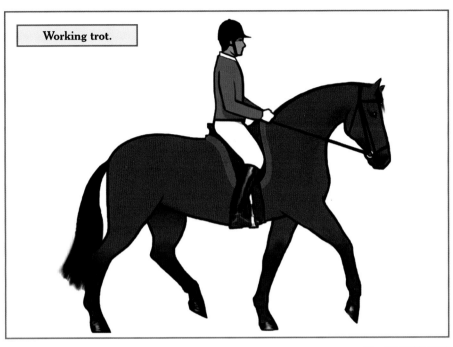

Working trot.

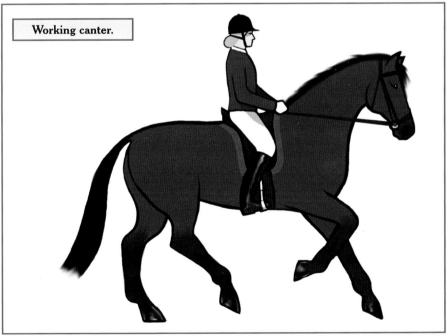

Working canter.

The rider should maintain a correct position whilst making transitions.

The Weight Aids

The rider's body rhythm has tremendous influence over the horse. By regulating your own body rhythm, you can quicken or slow down the step. For instance, if the horse is trying to rush forward at trot you must be able to control the speed at which you are rising at the trot so you are not relying totally on the hand. Do not let the horse intimidate you and make you rush along with it.

Your seat should remain soft and absorb the movement through the hip. Never sit down and drive the horse forward with an overactive seat. Feel the horse stepping up to you and allow it that freedom through the back.

The Half Halt

The half halt is applied with the outside rein. It is steadying the pace if the horse is bounding forward too much or as you are preparing for a downward transition of pace. Your legs must stay in constant contact with the horse's body so that it is taught to step forwards in the downward transition. The half halt prepares it for this so that it is not suddenly surprised by a strong active hand that hauls it back. It is also used to regulate the pace to help keep the horse in a rounded, elastic frame.

Transitions

Halt to Walk: The horse must be attentive, accept the contact and look straight ahead. Ask the horse to step forward by closing both legs on its sides. As it steps forward, allow your arms to follow the movement of its head and neck while still maintaining an elastic contact. Do not push the young horse out of rhythm at the walk by trying to go too fast. It will learn to walk out in time, especially if you are able to go out with another horse around the tracks and lanes.

Walk to Trot: Shorten the reins if necessary as the young horse may be in a longer frame at the walk. Close both legs on its sides on the girth area. Use your voice if needed and as the horse steps into the trot encourage a forward step by maintaining contact with your lower legs. The head and neck do not show as much movement as in the walk, but encourage the horse to stretch forward and down in an elastic frame to allow the withers and shoulders more freedom. Maintain the correct lateral flexion at all times.

Trot to Canter: If the young horse is sufficiently balanced on the trot, and before you try to ride it at canter, it should be cantered on the lunge. I would recommend only short moments in canter. The horse can learn the command to canter from the trainer's voice aids, and learn to balance itself without the worry of carrying the rider as well. Keep the side reins long and in a steady contact. Ideally, the field is the best place to teach the horse to canter; the going needs to be firm but not hard. Space is needed so that the horse is not continually having to turn. It will find 20 x 40m (64 x 13ft) a very small area in which to learn to canter. Make sure the horse is obedient and under control when walking and trotting before you ask for canter in the field. Over a period of time it will learn to balance itself and be able to shorten its step to cope with a smaller area. The inexperienced rider should not attempt to ride the young horse at canter in large, open spaces.

To make the transition from trot to canter the horse must be sufficiently active but not too fast to strike off. Maintain the correct outline and ask the horse to canter on a curve to the right or left. If you are in an enclosed area ask for the canter on the first corner of the short side where you begin to curve around the corner, presenting the horse in the correct bend.

Keep the inside leg on the girth. Apply the half halt if needed and ask for the canter by bringing the outside leg just a little behind the girth. Maintain the canter with

Behind the vertical.

Behind the contact.

False bend - flexion is from a point behind the poll.

Leaning on the bit.

Against the hand, above the bit.

the inside leg and allow freedom of the head and neck. If correctly presented, the horse should strike off onto the correct leg. The horse canters in three-time: 1 outside hind; 2 inside hind and outside fore together; 3 inside fore leading leg.

Canter to Trot: Prepare the horse in canter using the half halt and give it good time to adjust the step so that it gradually steadies the canter into the trot. Establish a good rhythm as soon as it regains its balance and do not let it walk until you feel the trot is correct. It may take a little time to feel as good in trot after canter as it did before canter but the horse has to learn to adjust its stride and this will take time.

Trot to Walk: Make sure the horse is trotting forward rhythmically with an elastic contact. The pace must feel right. Apply the half halt to prepare for walk. Keep your legs in close contact to maintain the energy in the step. Use the outside rein to ask the horse to walk but allow it time to alter the step. You should feel that you are moving forward from the trot to the walk and therefore your hand allows the horse to alter the head and neck and stretch forward to a yielding arm. Do not increase your leg aid from walk, simply maintain the leg and only ask for the walk when the trot is forward. Try not to use too much rein in the downward transition, causing the horse to resist and upset its balance. Encourage the horse to step forward as it makes the transition down.

Walk to Halt: Use the half halt and give the horse time to alter its step in response to the aid. Ask for the halt with the outside rein and voice. The young horse needs time to understand the aids, so repeat a gentler motion rather than make the hand stronger.

In Summary

A great deal of time and patience is needed to train the horse to make good transitions. Only ask for a transition when the pace you are in is correct. Give the horse space to move: away from the corners or on a large circle is preferable to the short side of the arena or in a corner.

Chapter Five

Basic school movements

In your schooling sessions, try to use varied and interesting school movements rather than going continuously on a circle or around the track. Of course, a certain amount of work needs to be learned on the 20m (60ft) circle to help open the shoulders and perfect the lateral flexion but do not overdo this in the early stages.

The young horse needs to learn to stay straight on the circle, hind legs following forelegs or stepping into the line of the forehand. See lateral flexion on page 9.

The 20-metre Circle

The 20-metre circle may be started at the A, C, B or E markers in the 20 x 40m school. The centre circle makes it less easy for the horse to maintain straightness because it has so much open space around it. When riding a 20-metre circle at A or C, imagine a square that takes up half the school with a line from the corner to the centre marker, across the centre line and up the other side. Draw an imaginary cross in the square. Picture and note the points at which the lines hit the track. Start the circle at A or C and ride a curved line to the half way point between the corner and the centre marker, hit the track, take one step and continue in another curved line to the centre of the school and so on until you return to A or C. Dividing the circle into four equal arcs makes it far easier to negotiate a correct shape.

Common Faults

1. Allowing the horse to drift.
2. Riding an oval shape.
3. Incorrect flexion leading to crookedness.

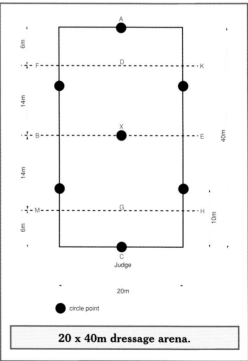

20 x 40m dressage arena.

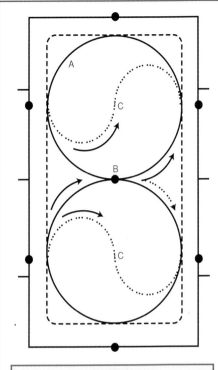

A: Circle
B: Change of rein out of the circle
C: Change of rein through circle.

Common Faults

1. Allowing the horse to drift too far down the school making the circle too big.
2. Not keeping the circle central.
3. Incorrect lateral flexion.

Turns

Various turns are used to enable the horse to change direction whilst continuing to move correctly and maintain rhythm. Therefore it is vital to give the horse room and be aware of where you are leaving and returning to the track.

Diagonal Line

This is a simple turn allowing the horse maximum freedom through the corners. Do not attempt to push the young horse too deeply into the corners as it will be insufficiently shortened at this stage of training.

1. Leave the track just after your shoulders pass the corner marker.
2. Turn and look to a point a stride before the diagonal marker.
3. Maintain a continuous flexion and change that flexion just before you reach the diagonal marker to change the rein. You can change the flexion in the centre of the school but I would rather wait until the horse reaches the track.
4. Apply the half halt before change of flexion.

4. Too much inside bend allowing the withers to slip to the outside, losing straightness.

When riding the 20-metre circle in the centre of the school at markers B or E, it is easier to imagine this circle in two halves. Leave the track a stride after B, turn your shoulders slightly and look round towards E. Hit the track one stride before that marker and leave the track one stride past it, looking forward to B. Cross the centre line exactly half way between X/A and D/C.

Change of Rein out of the 20-metre Circle

Ride a half 20-metre circle from A to X. Apply the half halt a few strides before X, change the flexion and reverse the aids. Continue on a correct arc from X to the track.

Common Faults

1. Riding a diagonal line instead of two half circles.
2. Forgetting to change the flexion and therefore falling in on the change of rein.
3. Uneven half circles not stepping through X.

Turn Across the Centre Line

Ask the horse to leave the track approximately its own body length before the centre line marker. Look across the school well before you turn in order to track onto the centre line rather than fall past it. Apply the half halt before you turn. Keep the legs in close contact to remind the horse to maintain a rhythmical step. You may either change the rein or stay on the same rein but there should be a difference between a turn across the centre line and a half circle turn from the 20-metre circle. Apply the half halt before and after change of direction if necessary. Remember to give the horse room to turn before reaching the opposite marker; again it will need its own body length in which to turn.

Common Faults

1. Turning too late or too early.
2. Falling across on a half circle line.
3. No change of flexion or overbending of the neck.
4. Losing the rhythm on the turns.

Turn Down the Centre Lane

This is one of the more difficult turns as it is only 10m from the corner to the centre line so this needs careful riding and plenty of practice.

Prepare for the turn by maintaining correct flexion as you leave the track a horse's body length in front of the marker. A definite half halt should be applied to prepare the horse. Turn and look down the centre line to the far marker and keep the horse straight. Change the rein or remain on the same rein but remember to tell the horse which way you are going a horse's length before the marker.

Common Faults

1. Riding the turn too fast or too slow.
2. No preparation, that is, omitting the half halt.
3. Turning too late or too early.
4. Not looking where you are going.
5. Incorrect flexion or too much neckbend.

Most of the common faults that occur when riding turns and circles are caused by the rider's basic aids being incorrect and, therefore, the horse not understanding the command. Whether you are riding a turn or a circle, the horse must remain straight, in the correct flexion with all the basic principles being adhered to.

Diagonals

The rider should sit on the correct diagonal at all times, remembering to change the diagonal when changing the rein. Sit when the horse's inside hind and outside fore legs are on the ground. Your inside leg is on the girth and may be applied (as you sit) to encourage the horse's inside hind to step forwards. Those who only want to hack still need to change the diagonal regularly to prevent the horse from becoming one-sided. Your body weight being continually carried on one diagonal pair of legs will eventually alter the balance and give a twisted feeling under the saddle.

Loops

The young horse needs to come away from the sides of the school, particularly if you are working in an enclosed area. Sometimes ride it on the inner track or ride shallow loops. Ask the horse to leave the track as your shoulders pass the corner marker. Imagine a post 3m away from the back at the centre line marker. Change the flexion so that the horse curves around the imaginary post. Change the flexion as you return to negotiate the corner correctly. You should return a horse's stride before the marker, having ridden a continuous curved line which is equal in width either side of the centre marker. Apply the half halt when necessary.

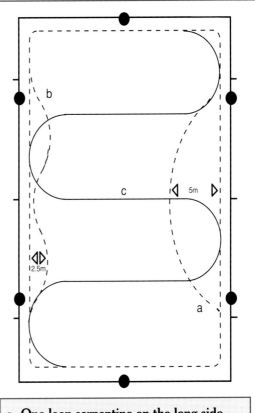

a. **One loop serpentine on the long side.**
b. **Two loop on the long side.**
c. **Four loop serpentine across the whole school.**

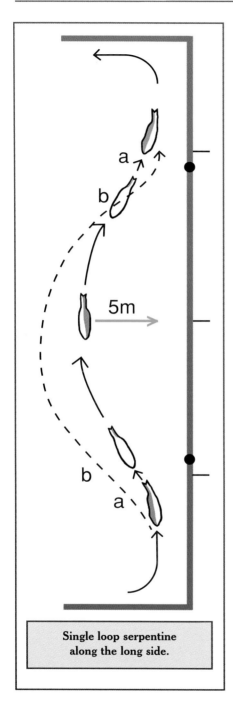

Single loop serpentine along the long side.

Serpentines

The horse is asked to cross the school in a series of half circle shapes. In a 20 x 40m school the horse will cross the centre line twice, making three half circles. Each half circle will measure just over 13m. The rider must know this so that the serpentine can be ridden accurately. A change of bend should be asked as the horse crosses the centre line by a change of aids and turn of the rider's body. A definite half halt is used to warn the horse of the intended movement. Each half circle shape should be the same. Often the middle half circle becomes too large or is ridden in a triangular shape. The horse should cross the centre line parallel to the short sides of the school before the change of flexion into the next bend. The young horse at this stage will learn to become more balanced working on a smaller area. Do not attempt this movement until it is balanced on the 20-metre circle.

In conclusion

These are all simple movements but need to be established before moving on to smaller circles and more advanced turns. The horse is working at preliminary level. Later on, it will develop the ability to shorten and lengthen its stride and move away from the leg. Establish the basics and you are on the right road to more complex and advanced works. Remember to progress in the horse's own time and keep it happy. Riding is for pleasure and it should be so for both horse and rider.

Glossary

Activity - Power within the stride

Half halt - Steadying of the pace

Impulsion - Controlled energy

Loop - Technical term used for a curved line along the side of the school

Moving straight - Hindlegs to follow in the track of the forelegs

Neck rein - Strap around the horse's neck for the rider to hold

Overbend - Going too deep; behind the vertical

Pommel - Front of the saddle

Rhythm - Regular step

Rising trot - Lift of the rider's seat in time with the horse's trot

Serpentine - A continuous curved line in equal parts across the school

Transition - Change of pace

Tempo - Speed

Weight aids - Body rhythm and the influence of the rider's seat and back

Index